The
Himalayan Journey of
BUDDHISM

The Himalayan Journey of BUDDHISM

NANCY MOORE GETTELMAN

SEATTLE / MILWAUKEE

Library of Congress Number: 89-92258

ISBN 0-9624427-0-4

Photographs by Nancy Moore Gettelman
and Rev. Richard Sherburne, S.J.

A complete list of credits is included on page 96.

Printed in the United States of America

PROCRUSTES PRESS
P.O. Box 691
Elm Grove, Wisconsin 53122

A west view of the Potala, red paint marks monastic portion of colossal structure.

CONTENTS

OPPOSITE — *Prayer flags on pathway leading to Tiger's Nest Monastery, Western Bhutan.*

Mount Kanchenjunga in background with Tibetan monstery in Bhutia Busti below.
Darjeeling in West Bengal, India.

FOREWORD

The purpose of this book is to provide guideposts for those interested in Buddhism, particularly the kind that evolved throughout the Himalayan kingdoms after it left its birthplace in India.

My interest in the subject began in 1953, when my husband received a gift of Lowell Thomas Jr.'s book, *Out of this World*, while in the hospital. I was fascinated to read about the Tibetans, so far from the world's mainstream, and it awoke a curiosity in me that has taken all these years to satisfy. I read all the popular books on the subject of "mysterious Tibet," and wished someday to be able to go there. Thirty-three years later, in 1986, that wish was fulfilled.

In the meantime, however, that abiding interest led me down by-ways that have greatly enriched my life, and questions were answered that for years were perplexing to this western mind. Throughout the text I have tried to share with the searching reader.

The answers came from a variety of sources. One was the acquiring of an advanced degree in Tibetan Buddhist Studies in 1973 from the University of Wisconsin, after attending the two universities. The first was the University of British Columbia at Vancouver, where once a week for two years I made a seven-hour, round-trip by car and ferry from Victoria, B.C., where my husband and I were living at the time. When we moved to Milwaukee, I transferred to the University of Wisconsin to study under Geshe Lhondup Sopa, driving the eighty miles to Madison twice a week for a year. My commuting brought a few tolerant smiles!

Another source was the opportunity to travel and see first-hand the things I had read about, and to place them in context. This travel was tremendously enriched by several Canadian Jesuit friends in India and in the Himalayan kingdoms, who have lived there for years as teachers. I had met a number of them while I was Foreign Student Counselor at Marquette University in Milwaukee and they were visiting the Jesuit colleges in North America during their home leave. Their kindness and hospitality can never be measured or repaid.

I want to thank Father Richard Sherburne, S.J., professor of Buddhist Studies at Seattle University, for the use of many of his beautiful slides as well as his consultation and affirmation throughout the writing of the text; Roz Pape at Murray Publishing Co. for not only her artistic layout of this book, but her encouragement throughout the months of preparation; and my husband, Tom, for his continuing interest in these endeavors. Without the cooperation of these important people, I would never have been able to complete this work.

—Nancy Moore Gettelman
Seattle/Milwaukee

INDIA

ANCIENT INDIA

The history of Buddhism is rooted in the pre-Hindu culture of India which extends as far back as 2500 B.C. when great masses of Indo-Europeans (the original Caucasians) were moving out of the Black Sea area. Some tribes settled in Greece; some migrated as far as Asia Minor and Persia. Still others, calling themselves Aryans (Sanskrit for "noble ones"), pushed on to northwest India through the Khyber, continued eastward to the Punjab, and on down into the Gangetic plain.

The Aryans were nomadic herdsman, so there are no material traces of their earlier times. The only "artifact" of their wandering culture is the collection of oral religious traditions known as the *Vedas*. These four books give their name to the Vedic period (1500 B.C.-500 A.D.).

The oldest and most important of the collection is the *Rig Veda*, composed of about 1000 hymns addressed to their many deities, who parallel the Olympian gods and goddesses of the ancient Greeks. A study of the *Rig Veda* reveals that were no temples. The brahmin priests offered ritual sacrifices in open spaces to such gods as Agni, god of fire; Soma, the liquid poured in oblation; Indra, god of war. The Vedic Aryans had no clear belief in rebirth, nor of afterlife in a "heaven" and "hell." They were concerned only with the here and now.

Over the centuries, the Aryan conquest and absorption of earlier civilizations in India made their society increasingly complex. Wandering tribes were now settled into small kingdoms,

TOP — *Shiva, god of both destruction and fecundity, is here depicted as patron of yogins, with Mother Ganges streaming out of his head, his blue skin signifying divinity.*

ABOVE — *The Kashmiri Gate in the walls surrounding Old Delhi, built by the Mogul emperor, Shah Jehan. A Hindu sadhu passes on his begging rounds.*

OPPOSITE — *The future Buddha Maitreya holding his hands in the "earth-witnessing" gesture.*

Khyber Pass: Beginning 11 miles west of Peshawar, Pakistan, this narrow passage winds for 33 miles between shale and limestone cliffs of the Hindu Kush down into Afghanistan. In 1500 BC the Aryans came through, subjugating the indigenous Indus Valley civilization, and over the centuries other groups, such as the Persians, White Huns, Mughals, and the British followed, leaving their mark on India.

tribal chiefs became kings, and a caste system developed with these levels: Priest-Noble-Merchant-Worker. Three new fundamental concepts of Indian thought came into being as well: (a) *karma* — the natural law of moral retribution which rationalized the caste system, (b) *samsara* — the cycle of transmigrations and reincarnations, and (c) *dharma* — the duty by which one is bound according to his present caste. If one does his caste duty well, he will have a better rebirth. [See box, page 13]

By the sixth century B.C., a collection of philosophic treatises called the *Upanishads* emerged. These were the reflections of *rishis* (seers) who had abandoned what they felt was the empty outward ritual of the brahmins and, instead, sought to experience the truth within themselves. They also recognized a personal soul *(atman),* explored its relationship with the Universal Soul, Brahman, and probed into the means of liberation from the rebirth cycle. These speculations of the Upanishadic sages set the tone for all further religious development in India. The foundations of Hinduism were laid.

HINDUISM:

As Hinduism enveloped the land's dissimilar peoples, absorbing and processing their beliefs and philosophies, it was resilient, not dogmatic. There was no single form of worship prescribed, no single creed to be professed, and no single prophet to help the soul reach liberation.

Hindu thinkers came to regard the countless gods as manifestations of one single Absolute Being, Brahman. They believed that the ultimate divine Oneness which lies behind the universe shows three faces or functions to humans. As Brahma, he creates the universe; as Vishnu, he preserves what Brahma has created; and as Shiva, he destroys in order that new life may appear in the cosmic renewal process. Unlike Brahma, both Shiva and Vishnu were given human form, and today have millions of followers.

The aim of the Hindu is to escape the rebirth cycle and let his soul be reabsorbed into Brahman, the Universal Soul. To accomplish this liberation, Hindus believe there are Three Paths. (a) Path of Works (*karma*): observance of all moral precepts and caste rules (e.g., marriage, diet, initiation). (b) The Path of Devotion (*bhakti*): choosing one's own special deities (such as Vishnu, Shiva, etc.), reciting prayers and making offerings (*puja*) to them, in exchange for their help in life. (c) Ultimately, the Path of Knowledge (*jñāna*) is the way that must be followed; that is, by practicing Yoga one must see for oneself the true nature of Supreme Brahman and thereby become reabsorbed into it. That is Nirvana.

A leper pleading for alms.

KARMA AND REBIRTH

Karma. Buddha held to two Hindu doctrines, karma and rebirth, though he modified them. In the Law of Karma he held that a man of any caste could experience such a change of heart (in his wish for Awakening) that he might escape the full consequences of sins committed in past lives. One who is not subject to rebirth is one who has completely destroyed all cravings and exhausted old karma from previous existences. No new karma is being produced and there is no longing for a future life. Therefore, he is extinguished at death, like a lamp. It is only those who are not emancipated from "the will-to-live and have" who will be reborn.

Rebirth. Buddha gave that doctrine a form that is obscure and profound. He said that rebirth takes place without any actual soul-substance passing over from one existence to another.

Dharma. The dutiful way of life, according to the code of the caste one was born into. Dharmas are different for different people. By doing his duty correctly, a person affects his karma and will be born into better lives during the cycle of rebirths.

A woman sells an ear of roasted corn at a sidewalk "restaurant" in Delhi.

BUDDHISM:

Many thinkers of that Upanishadic period engaged in philosophical explorations, challenging the brahmins' powerful hold on popular belief and ritual observance. The greatest of these challengers appeared in the 7th century B.C. A charismatic figure, Siddhartha Gautama, broke with tradition and rejected the Hindu scriptures and caste system.

Siddhartha Gautama was the world's first and only religious leader to deny the concept of a soul. He was also the world's first psychologist and said that to find answers to life's problems one must look within, instead of reaching out to a saving God.

Born to a petty Hindu king who feared a prophecy that his son would either become a world ruler or an ascetic, Gautama lived in pro-

tected luxury, away from the harsh realities of life.

The legend of the Four Sights explains his religious calling. The young prince, riding outside the palace, saw in turn four men — one old and decrepit, one sickly, one dead, and finally a yellow-robed mendicant carrying a begging bowl, looking unmistakenly serene. From these sights

ABOVE — *Along the Jumna River ("Twin" of the Ganges) a woman fashions patties from cow and buffalo dung, which are then dried on the wall behind her, stacked, and sold for fuel.*

UPPER LEFT — *A bicycle-drawn rickshaw carries Muslim women in purdah.*

TRIPITAKA

The Tripitaka (Three Baskets) is the name given the collection of scriptures formed immediately after the Buddha's death. The name "Basket" indicates the container used to collect the loose palm leaves which were India's original "writing paper". The three collections are: *Vinaya* (Monks' Discipline), *Sutra* (Sermons), and *Abhidharma* (after-Teaching). Mahayana added hundreds of Sutras of its own, authored by celestial Buddhas and Bodhisattvas such as Maitreya, and delivered to unnamed holy men who disseminated them.

LEFT — *A sadhu begs from shop to shop, with the omnipresent cow in foreground. The cow is revered in India, not worshipped, for all its life-sustaining qualities.*

Gautama realized the fact of old age, sickness and death. But from the last sight, he learned that man could find peace by withdrawing from the world. Shortly afterward, he left his wife and baby son and crept away from the palace in the middle of the night, determined to find the real meaning of life. This is known as the "Great Renunciation".

At first, in the traditional way of spiritual seekers, he sat at the feet of gurus and listened to the wisdom of the *Upanishads*. Still unsatisfied, he joined a group of five ascetics who imposed great austerities on themselves. But, after six years of this, he collapsed from hunger, saved only by a village girl who happened by. Gautama then realized he needed his body in order to use his head to gain enlightenment. Abandoning all bodily mortification, he turned to solitary meditation, causing his companions to give him up in disgust.

For forty-nine days he sat meditating in yoga fashion under a tree near Benares. [See box, p. 17] During his absorption he saw the condition of mankind very clearly and understood why he had failed until now to experience release from suffering and to reach liberation. By that experience, Siddhartha Gautama became the Buddha, the "Awakened One".

What was it that Buddha "awakened" to?

He realized that human suffering and conflict

The Wheel and two reclining deer symbolize Buddha's first sermon in the Deer Park at Benares, where he first "turned the "Wheel of the Law."

A woman of the Shudra caste carries a heavy load up a bamboo scaffolding.

ORDER OF CASTE SYSTEM IN INDIA
TODAY (now outlawed)
1. BRAHMIN
2. WARRIOR
3. MERCHANT
4. LABORER
5. OUTCASTE

Boy monks at the doorway of Swayambhunath shrine in Kathmandu, Nepal.

YOGA, MEDITATION:

The yoga meditation technique Siddhartha was following is the ancient method of concentration for self awareness. In order to arrive at the realization of one's true and real self, one practices a psycho-analysis which can eliminate all subconscious false self-images. It was, however, for the Buddha the greater realization that there is no "real self", but only "Buddha-nature", the emptiness (absence of) of a so-called "self".

There are four levels of concentration (*samadhi*) in Yoga:

4. Intuitive:
   Self-realization only. ⎫
   ⎬ HIGHER
3. Intuitive:
   Joy of self-experiencing. ⎭
2. Conceptual:
   Analytical, reflective. ⎫
   ⎬ LOWER
1. Conceptual:
   Simple focus on object. ⎭

The Buddha had already achieved the highest level of self insight and knowledge, common to all yogins (yoga meditators) and well-adjusted persons. But he went *further* when he perceived that even clinging to the idea of a supposed "true self" still left the individual tied to this world and its potential for suffering. By letting go of even *that* clinging, he achieved the fullest Awakening and escaped the rebirth-cycle. He then passed into a state of supreme "wakefulness." That *is* Nirvana.

CHAIN OF DEPENDENT ORIGINATION

DEPENDENT ORIGINATION or Law of "Causation" behind the cycle of rebirth.

Suffering comes out of a twelve-linked chain of "causes and effects." The first two belong to the previous life, the middle eight belong to the present, and the last two to the future existence. Only in links 1. (Ignorance) and 8 (Desire) can the chain be broken, where one has the choice of overcoming ignorance and of letting go of desire. Buddha proclaimed that there is no real causation, but only relativity, which is the basis for the Buddhist belief in the interdependence of all things.

PREVIOUS LIFE
1. The cause of being born is *Ignorance* (as stated in the Four Holy Truths) which is the setting for
2. *Predispositions* from the karma of previous existences. The karmic characteristics determine the quality of:

PRESENT LIFE
3. *Consciousness* which determines the:
4. *Name and form:* particular physical traits of the individual which lead to
5. The *Six Senses* (the usual five senses plus mind) which in turn make:
6. *Contact* with their objects;
7. From which *Sensation* or feeling arises, which in turn causes:
8. *Desire* (or thirst, craving). From craving comes:
9. *Clinging* to existence (so as to continue the pleasure or cease the displeasure).
10. This is the *Becoming* process toward the new

FUTURE LIFE
11. *Birth* which must include
12. *Old age,* and *Death.*

were caused by ignorance of one's real self. This meant two things. First, in the psychological sense, we create pseudo-selves and play roles which lead to conflict. And second, the ultimate cause of all suffering lies in the desire (craving, grasping, clinging) for a real self-identity, which of necessity is constantly thwarted because, in actuality, "self" has no true existence.

Buddha's reflection on the cause of suffering through life-after-life was in terms of a then current quasi-philosophical description of the process of rebirth, called the Chain of Dependent Origination. [See box, p. 17]. It is a more detailed explanation of how karma works in the process of the next body's rebirth.

Now, having "exhausted" his karma, Buddha could enter Nirvana (Liberation) at his death. He wondered whether or not to remain simply at peace within himself or to become a Teacher for everyone, explaining the path he himself had found.

He decided to go forth. In the Deer Park outside the holy city of Benares, he gave his first sermon (sutra), known as the "Turning of the Wheel of the Teaching". His only audience was the band of five ascetics with whom he had once practiced extreme mortification.

To them Buddha proclaimed the Middle Way, saying that neither a life of extreme indulgence nor one of extreme mortification was the way to live. The only answer to suffering lay in the Four Noble Truths and Eightfold Path. [See box, p. 21] Following them would lead to Nirvana. His teaching (dharma) was later summarized as having Three Marks (or characteristics): Suffering, Impermanence, and No-Soul. Buddha challenged his former companions to believe his testimony and to try the Middle Way. They were converted, and thus the Sangha (the Buddhist monastic community) came into being. It was the first order of celibate monks in the world. The single state — so contrary to traditional Hindu ideals and values — was enjoined for the sake of

ABOVE RIGHT — *On road to Agra a travelling entertainer with his bear.*

OPPOSITE TOP — *A town near Bombay.*

OPPOSITE BOTTOM — *A sidewalk tea vendor washing cups at the curb.*

BODHISATTVAS

There are two kinds of Bodhi-sattvas (Sanskrit:"Awakening-Being"):

1. Great Bodhisattvas: the timeless, already awakened Buddhas such as Maitreya, Avalokita, Amitabha, etc.
2. Ordinary Bodhisattvas: those who are still striving for Bodhi or returning to help others. The Bodhisattva Vow is unique in its noble compassion, and taken by layman and monk alike; it has three parts —
   a) To seek Awakening (insight);
   b) But for the sake of other creatures; not oneself
   c) And to defer one's Nirvana and continue to return in life after life in order to help others achieve Nirvana, until all sentient beings are finally awakened. Then this world of illusion will cease to exist.

19

religious community, and for the life of meditation and study.

As membership in the monastic Sangha grew, it was governed by definite rules laid down by the Buddha. These are known as the Vinaya ("Discipline"). After noviceship, years of study and spiritual training, the monk took some 250 additional vows pertaining to observance of poverty, the celibate state, etiquette, and rules for preserving harmony in the monasteries.

The Sangha with its no-caste distinction — a revolutionary concept and challenge to traditional Hindu society — soon attracted many dedicated followers. Thus the Sangha was enlarged to include householders (married followers) as well as monks. Both groups subscribed to the Three Jewels or Three Refuges: "I take refuge (from suffering) in the Buddha, in the Dharma, and in the Sangha." It was largely due to the householders' generosity that the Sangha acquired its monasteries (or viharas: dwelling places for monks, used mainly during the rainy season), some of them quite extensive.

Originally Buddhism was an ethic and philosophy, not a religion. Buddha did not want to be worshipped. He thought of himself as a "guide" along the path to liberation from samsara. Intensely practical, he rejected philosophical speculation as the way to liberation. He felt it was pointless to discuss what could not be proven, such as evidence for or against a Creator. Buddha's only concern was that we are here now, and we are suffering now. And he showed each disciple how to rely on his own powers.

However, by the 3rd century B.C., an important divergence of interpretation occurred from which emerged the two great Buddhist schools, *Theravada* (Elder's Way) and *Mahayana* (Greater Vehicle) — for getting to Nirvana.

Theravada (also known as Hinayana — Lesser Vehicle) is closer to Buddha's original teaching. Its emphasis is on Wisdom (seeing the "no-soul" of persons), [See box, p. 20] and is directed towards the seeking of liberation for oneself alone. Its followers adhere to the formula of the Three Jewels and their goal is to achieve Nirvana as Arhats (saints), never hoping to be Buddhas themselves. They recognize only one Buddha, the historical human teacher, Siddhartha Gautama. Theravada spread from India to Sri Lanka, Burma and throughout southeast Asia.

In Mahayana, Buddhist philosophy and ethical doctrines were slowly transformed into a religion. External manifestations such as beliefs in rites, images, and supra-natural powers were introduced. In addition to Theravada's Wisdom, Mahayanists believe in "Emptiness" (*sunyata*),

BUDDHA'S NO-SOUL DOCTRINE

A person has no soul (*anatman*), but rather what we call the "self" is merely a composition of phenomena grouped as the Five Heaps (*skandhas*): (1) Body, (2) Feelings, (3) Perception, (4) Predispositions — a lumping together of the instincts and the subconscious impressions, and (5) consciousness.

The ego is only an "appearance" because at death the union of the Five Heaps is dissolved. Therefore, the ego is only a name we give to the functional unity that subsists when the Five Heaps set up the complex interplay that constitutes the personal life of the individual.

The Heaps are composed of phenomena (point-instants of energy) in perpetual flux, and taken together are called the "conscious stream." It is one's conscious stream, with its karmic coloring or conditioning, which transmigrates, Buddha said.

The comparison is often made to a seal being pressed upon wax. The characters, engraved on the seal and retained by the wax, are what pass over. There is nothing substantial — no "soul" passes over.

Old and new in ancient India.

which means that everything, even the phenomena of the conscious stream of a person, is devoid of its "own-being." It is dependent on other things for existence and can exist only in its relationship with them. As Buddha explained in the Chain of Dependent Origination, everything is relative.

Unlike the Theravadins, Mahayanists believe that there are countless Buddhas, beside Siddhartha Gautama, and that all sentient beings are potentially Buddhas (fully Awakened Ones). For the attainment of Nirvana, Compassion for all creatures became as important as Wisdom. Thus the Mahayanists developed the doctrine of the "Bodhisattva." [See box, p. 19].

Mahayana spread to China, Korea, Japan, Nepal, Tibet, Sikkim and Bhutan.

DECLINE OF BUDDHISM IN INDIA:

After the seventh century A.D., Buddhism started to decline in India. There were many causes. One was the separation of the monks from the rest of society in pursuit of their own liberation. They performed few of the life-enveloping ceremonies the Brahmins did, yet they depended on the community to feed them. Another cause was the all-embracing aspect of later Hinduism, which absorbed many of the Buddha's teachings. Invasions of northern India by the White Huns in the sixth century, and tribes of the Islamic faith from the eight century on, contributed to Buddhism's demise as well. Libraries and universities were destroyed. Many monks were killed or fled north to Nepal and Tibet.

FOUR NOBLE TRUTHS:

The First Noble Truth is that life is SUFFERING: birth is suffering; death is suffering; having what we dislike is suffering; losing what we love is suffering.

The Second Noble Truth is that suffering has an ORIGIN. This origin lies in human beings clinging to ignorance: seeking permanence in what is impermanent, pleasure in what is finally unpleasant, self-identity in what is not really one's self.

The Third Noble Truth is that there can be a CEASING of these origins of suffering. Ignorance can be seen, overcome, and rooted out.

The Fourth Noble Truth is the EIGHTFOLD PATH which is the means to rooting out our ignorance: changing our outlook and finding new patterns of behavior which will eventually result in Awakening.

The steps of the Eightfold Path are:

1. RIGHT VIEWS — clearly understanding the cause of one's illness.

2. RIGHT PURPOSE — deciding that one wants to be cured.

3. RIGHT SPEECH and

4. RIGHT CONDUCT — together aim at being cured.

5. RIGHT LIVELIHOOD — doing nothing to interfere with one's aim of being cured.

6. RIGHT EFFORT — sustaining the process that will bring desired results.

7. RIGHT AWARENESS — incessant examination of one's symptoms, tracing them to their cause, and removing the cause of the symptoms.

8. RIGHT CONCENTRATION or MEDITATION, so that one's focus on the cause is seen deeply.

Monks in Darjeeling.

NEPAL

According to geologists, millions of years ago India was an island separated from the Asian mainland. The force of their eventual contact pushed up the Himalayan mountains, which would explain the ancient sea fossils found at 9000 feet in Nepal. Kathmandu Valley, a 15 by 20 mile flat oval in the center of the country, was once a lake, evident in the layer of sludge under its surface. The rest of this beautiful, rectangular country is a staircase of terraced mountainsides. Beginning with the Terai, a tropical strip of the Ganges plain, fertile steps lead up to the highest peaks of the Himalaya, and on to remote Tibet.

The first rulers of Kathmandu Valley were the Kirati kings, who emigrated from the eastern part of Nepal at about the time of the Buddha (7th century B.C.). They were replaced by the Licchavis (400 A.D. to 700 A.D.), the same people as those of Vaisali, in Bihar. The Licchavi dynasty began the rule of Hindu kings, although they did not impose their religion on their Buddhist subjects. Nepal is still the only country where Hinduism is the state religion, the monarchs being considered reincarnations of Vishnu.

In 602 A.D., Amsuvarman, not a Licchavi, inherited the throne from his father-in-law and founded the Thakuri dynasty. According to Tibetan chronicles, it was Amsuvarman's daughter who married the powerful Tibetan king, Srong-tsan-gampo. She and his other wife, a Chinese princess, are known as the two aspects of Tara (the Buddhist goddess of compassion), because they converted Srong-tsan-gampo to Buddhism. It is interesting to note, however, that this event does not appear in the Nepali records — historians observing that a priori no Hindu would have given his daughter to a Tibetan, a non-Hindu.

It was the Thakuri dynasty that consolidated

OPPOSITE — *Terraced hillsides approaching Kathmandu Valley.*

the independence of Nepal — still only Kathmandu Valley — by setting up trade agreements on an equal status with India, Tibet, and China.

Towards the beginning of the 13th century, the Muslim conquest of northern India and the consequent establishment of Islamic sultans and kings in Delhi and Agra, caused many Indian princes, particularly from Rajasthan, to flee the country. In order to remain loyal to their Hindu faith, they went north and settled in the hilly areas of Nepal.

Although Hindus number about 90 percent of the population today, there is complete religious freedom for other creeds. In the course of Nepal's long history, religious differences have never caused a war. The followers of Buddhism, which came from India to Nepal in the third to fourth century A.D., account for about 15 percent of the people — Muslims only 1-2 percent.

Over the centuries, Hindus and Buddhists have intermingled to such an extent that they often celebrate the same festivals, worshipping the same deities, but with different understandings. Buddhist lay people followed the precepts of the dharma and supported the early monks. But they needed the Brahmins for worshipping the gods, and for life-cycle rituals, such as birth, marriage and death.

The form of Buddhism which became most popular in Nepal is Tantrayana, a variation of Mahayana. "The Path of the Tantras" is also known as Vajrayana, "the Path of the Thunderbolt," or "the Diamond Path." [See box, p. 24] Tantra is a Sanskrit word which means "thread," as used in the basic warp of weaving. Thus Tantra reinforces the Buddhist view of the basic interwovenness of the material and spiritual world.

Tantrism introduced a secret and very different approach to the goal of Enlightenment. Now "Awakening" was something that could be gained in the course of a single lifetime, instead of the slower path which took many rebirths. For this reason, Tantrayana has been referred to as the "swift path," as opposed to the "gradual path" of Mahayana.

A monkey sits next to a giant vajra at the head of the stairs to Swayambhunath stupa.

TANTRA-VAJRAYANA:

The sexual symbolism of higher Tantra involves the cult of the female energy, "shakti," (in Tibetan Buddhism called "prajna"). The shakti symbolizes the divine energy of Wisdom and is shown in the intimate embrace of a serene Bodhisattva, who represents Compassion. Sometimes sculptured, sometimes painted on a thankha, this Tantric art depicts the union of Wisdom and Compassion, necessary for entering Nirvana. It is not considered erotic as viewed by initiates who have attained the appropriate level of insight.

Tantrayana is also called Vajrayana or Diamond Path. Like a diamond, it is hard and unbreakable, capable of cutting all substances, but cannot itself be cut. Vajrayana's primary symbol is a scepter (Sanskrit: *vajra*, Tibetan: *dorje*), standing for Compassion. In ritual practice, it is held in the right hand, representing the male principle; while the left hand holds a hand-bell, the female counterpart of the scepter, symbolizing Wisdom. Relevant mudras are performed. The bell and dorje of each meditator are inseparable ritual partners in Tantric meditation.

MANDALAS are sacred diagrams drawn in colored sand on the ground or painted on canvas or walls. They are used as a tool in meditation or used ritually in the invoking of deities to grant super-human powers.

Their design is geometric — a circle within a square, representing the deity's dwelling place (the innermost part of the mandala). The deity is invoked in accordance with pre-

Mani Wall with the mantra, 'Om Mani Padme Hum."

scribed rites: using incense, offerings, and invocations. When the contemplator identifies himself with the deity, the deity's power is transferred to him.

The mandala's intricate system of colors, design and subject matter contains coded messages, communicable only to the initiate at certain levels of spiritual awareness.

MANTRAS are sacred words or syllables which embody a specific deity or supernatural power in the sounds. Uttering mantras is a way of aiding meditation. They are also necessary for getting in touch with one's already existing inner forces, as they carry spiritual empowerment with them. The recital of mantras is often accompanied by a hand bell and hand drum.

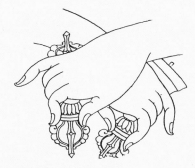

A Vajahankara mudra.

MUDRAS are symbolic hand movements used in rituals to accompany the mantras. Recalling the mantra with the mind, articulating it with the mouth, and presenting it physically with the mudra represent the three constituents of the human personality: body, speech, and mind.

VISUALIZATION is a form of meditation. It is the method through which the mantra and mandala are activated and their innate powers made real to the aspirant. Special visualizations are designed by the initiate's guru to suit the initiate's own nature and degree of personal understanding.

Transformation is the key word. Mudras, mantras and mandalas (body, speech and mind) help the aspirant become wholly concentrated and absorbed in his meditation, as he creates a mental vision of the deity with whom he seeks union. After he assumes the qualities of the deity, and understands them fully, he is transformed.

For the Vajrayana adept, the internal and external world are not separate (no duality). Consequently, there is no question of the "reality" of the mentally constructed deity. This is only another way of saying that Tantrayana/Vajrayana are solidly grounded in the basic Mahayana description of Emptiness.

The process of visualization proves that the mind is the preeminent power in the creation of reality.

Tantra is an elaboration of basic Yoga techniques of concentration. Mantras, mudras and mandalas [See box, p. 25] are used to attain the goal, conceived as a mystical union with basic Reality, which is non-dual. This Reality has two aspects which are symbolically expressed as a sexual union between a Bodhisattva (Compassion) and his female consort (Wisdom). [See box, p. 24].

Meditation on the symbol was intended to lead the devotee to an inner identification with the deity, and the transformation of the deity's powers to the devotee, which is supreme spiritual bliss. For these complicated rites one must first be initiated, then begin spiritual training with a qualified guru who stands in place of the Buddha, and who is able and willing to impart the truth of the secret texts. Otherwise, the words are meaningless. And misunderstanding of the techniques and symbolism can cause severe mental disorders.

Historically, Tantrayana often degenerated into ritual practices of a sexual or violent nature. Acting out the symbolism came to be substituted

for the insight which the symbols were intended to produce. Its roots are in India, but Tantrism is the most popular form of Buddhism in Bhutan, Ladakh, Mongolia, and Sikkim, as well as Nepal.

NEWARS:

The original inhabitants of Kathmandu Valley, the Newars, are thought to be a mixture of Mongoloid peoples from the north and Aryans from the south and west. About 10 percent are Buddhists.

Over the centuries, the Sanghas of the early Buddhist monasteries underwent a change in emphasis. The monks' vows of poverty, celibacy, and discipline (Vinaya), and their goal of study and meditation began to be replaced by the performance of Tantra and life cycle rituals for the people. The monks became married men with families. Each monastery was now open only to sons of members of the Sangha of that monastery (Newari: *baha*).

TOP — *Temple lions guard entrance to shrine at Kathmandu Baha (monastery).*

ABOVE — *A Newari Buddhist priest (vajracarya) conducts complicated ritual for devotees in front of a Swayambhunath shrine.*

OPPOSITE — *Newari woman selling silks and brass pots in bazaar near Kathmandu's Durbar Square.*

27

The Newari Buddhists are called Bare ("bah-ray"), and are divided into two groups:

a. *Sakya*: those who through initiation ritual belong to their father's sangha and its shrine, but are not empowered to perform rituals. (It is of interest that the initiation ceremony shows remnants of its monastic origins: the boys' take the monastic vows, have their heads shaved, and don monks' robes. After four days, they are "released" from their vows to lead lives as good Buddhist laymen.) The group's name is claimed from the clan of Siddhartha Gautama himself, "the Sage of Sakya," who was born in the Terai of Nepal.

b. *Vajracarya*: "Vajra-acarya" (Sanskrit for "Diamond-Teacher") is the title of a tantric ritualist. This group is considered higher than the Sakya because, in addition to the Bare initiation the Vajracarya undergo an empowerment ceremony enabling them to function as priests. They tend the shrines and perform religious ceremonies to the deities within and life-cycle rites for their client families.

The Bare became a caste in the 15th century when the Hindu king, Jyotir Malla, insisted that Buddhist society be organized along the lines of the Hindu caste system, probably for tax purposes.

The Bare are still considered a respected caste, both by themselves and by Hindus, equal or higher to the brahmins. The Sakyas and Vajracaryas engage in a variety of occupations, such as goldsmiths and silversmiths, stone workers, carpenters, masons, private business men, government employees, etc. At the present time, caste does not affect occupation. Unlike Hindu castes in India, both groups freely intermarry and interdine.

However, the caste structure of the Bare, especially the Vajracarya, presents a somewhat contradictory picture. On one hand, they are honored for their Buddhist religious tradition, which renounces caste; on the other, they are members of a Hindu society giving them a high caste status and certain social rewards based on their religious position.

Also, from the Buddhist point of view, the

King Bhupatindra Malla looking down on Hindu and Buddhist temples.

position of all Bare is inconsistent. The original Buddhist sangha was always democratic, open to persons of any class, race, or sex; whereas with Newar Buddhists, one can only become a Bare by birth. Their caste status seems likewise incongruous with the initiation rite that includes shaving the head — a Buddhist symbol of rejecting caste status.

THE MALLAS

In the early thirteenth century, there was one Muslim assault on the Kathmandu Valley. Temples were destroyed, images desecrated, and both Pashupatinath Temple and Swayambhunath Stupa were damaged.

The rulers of the valley from the thirteenth to eighteenth centuries were the Malla kings, descendants of refugees who fled to Nepal from northern India. They ruled by divine right as incarnations of Vishnu. Like the early Licchavis, the Malla dynasties followed strict Brahmin rituals. But they were tolerant of Buddhism which was widespread, especially in its Tantric form, Vajrayana.

A former Rana palace; now a Jesuit school, Godavari.

A number of the Malla kings were outstanding. Jaya Sthiti Malla, (1382-1422), who ruled from Bhaktapur (Bhadgaon), unified Kathmandu Valley which had been divided between three main cities, plus fragmented fiefdoms controlled by feudal lords. He also codified the caste system, emphasizing Brahmins as the highest social strata.

It was his son, Jyotir Malla (1422-1427), who imposed the caste status on Buddhist Newar society, otherwise allowing complete religious freedom.

By the fifteenth century distinctive Nepali-style art had developed, and most of the wood carving and sculpture seen today belongs to that period. A great supporter of the arts was Jyotir's son, Yaksa Malla (1428-1482). He also expanded his territory as far as the Ganges River in the south, the border of Tibet in the north, the Kali Gandaki in the west, and Sikkim in the east. Upon his death, his kingdom — Bhadgaon, Banepa, Patan, and Kathmandu — was divided among three daughters and a son. This was the beginning of destructive royal dissension.

As well as extending their territories, both Pratap and Bhupatindra Malla (1696-1722) were also patrons of art. They enhanced their cities with temples, pagodas, palaces, sewer systems, fountains and public baths — many of which are still to be seen.

But conflict among the kingdoms in Kathmandu Valley had gone on for almost two hundred years, and these political rivalries led to the Mallas' demise.

UNIFICATION OF NEPAL: THE SHAH DYNASTY

Gorkha (Gurkha), one of the many small kingdoms in the hills of western Nepal, was growing in strength under the rule of the ninth king of the Shah dynasty, Prithvi Narayan Shah. For years his Gurkha forces had been creeping closer to the valley, sealing it off, and causing economic pressure because of the loss of trade. Finally, early in the fall of 1768 on the night of the Indrajatra festival, the Gurkhas conquered the entire valley. The Malla age was over.

Prithvi Narayan Shah was the progenitor of modern Nepal. His ancestors were also Rajput princes who had fled the persecutions of the Muslim invaders in India. After moving to Kathmandu, he extended his territory from the Mahakali river in the West to the Sikkimese border in the East, approximately today's borders. He also brought the most important trade routes between India and Tibet under Shah control.

The regent, who governed during the minority of Prithvi Narayan Shah's grandson, repelled an invasion from Tibet. Then he counter-attacked, chased the invaders back to their own country, and took the town of Shigatse and its famous monastery, Tashilhunpo. To assist the Tibetans, the Ch'ing (Manchu) Emperor sent in troops. That assistance has importance to this day, with the Chinese claim that Tibet was always its vassal.

Between 1814-1816 the Gurkhas warred with the British, then ruling India. The British won Sikkim from Nepal and made it a protectorate, took most of the Terai, and posted a British Resident at Kathmandu. Distrustful of all foreigners after these events, the Nepalese rulers closed their borders until 1950.

The British, however, had been so impressed by the bravery of the Gurkhas that they began recruiting them into their own military service. Most of the men, famed for their tenacity and loyalty, were drawn from the hill tribes. They have served with the British and Indian armies, with mutual friendship and respect, through two World Wars and the Falkland Islands crisis.

RANAS

One of the most important eras in the history of Nepal was its rule by the usurping Ranas during the time the country was completely closed to outsiders.

Following a bloody coup in 1846, Jung Bahadur, an army general and member of the Rana clan, took over all political power, naming himself 'prime minister'. But he kept the legitimate prince, Surendra Bikram Shah, on the throne as a

OPPOSITE TOP — *Gurkhas during a religious festival. Thousands of goats are slaughtered for sacrificial purposes.*

RIGHT — *Monks looking at reliquary containing venerated stone which has a mantra naturally formed on it.*

OPPOSITE BOTTOM — *Brahmin of the Shiva shrine at Pashupatinath and his children.*

LEFT — *The stucco archway, showing Italian influence, leading to Bodhinath, supposedly the oldest shrine in Kathmandu Valley. Over the dome, the all-seeing eyes of compassionate Buddha gaze in the cardinal directions. According to legend, Bodhinath was founded by Boddhisattva Manjusri, who slashed the surrounding mountains with his sword, in order to drain the lake that once filled the valley.*

31

RIGHT — *A Buddha in earth-witnessing position with chortens in background.*

BELOW — *Swayambhunath ("self-born") stupa sits atop the single hill in Kathmandu Valley.*

ABOVE — *Earth-witnessing Buddhas flank the approach to Swayambhu, with small stone stupa offerings on the ground around.*

RIGHT — *Eyes of Hindu goddess Kali painted on stone at foot of stairs in Swayambhunath.*

OPPOSITE — *Spire of Swayambhu stupa, with colorful prayerflags strung from the pinnacle.*

figurehead, probably because of popular belief that the king is Vishnu's reincarnation.

Jung Bahadur declared his position as prime minister hereditary, and appointed family members to key posts in the army, administration, and government. Once his rule was firmly established, he traveled to England and France — an unorthodox thing to do in his day. Upon his return, he demonstrated his forward thinking by such acts as building several neo-classical palaces and abolishing the practice of *suttee*, the immolation of widows on their husbands' funeral pyres.

A later Rana prime minister abolished slavery and reformed the forced labor system introduced by the first Shah rulers. Another built schools.

In foreign affairs, the Ranas established good relations with British India. During the "Indian Mutiny" Nepal provided Gurkha military help, for which most of the Terai was returned to Nepal in 1860.

It was considered a relief to have some stability in government after generations of dissension in the royal family. But the greatest criticism of the Ranas is that while living lavishly themselves, they did not do enough for the country.

In 1950, the Indian government, alarmed by the Chinese invasion of eastern Tibet, and anxious to keep Nepal a strong, independent buffer state, assisted King Tribhuvan Shah, then living in New Delhi in voluntary exile, to mastermind and direct a successful revolt against the Rana regime.

Tribhuvan then returned to Nepal and, supported by the people, took up his legitimate reign. The present ruler is his grandson, King Birendra Bir Bikram Shah Dev.

SHERPAS

SHERPAS ("sher" means east, "pa" means person) are the best known of the high-Himalayan people and probably were no-madic tribes originally. Sometime between the 12th and 15th centuries they were driven south by the Mongol hordes, or by the warlike people of Kham in eastern Tibet. After being unsuccessful in their attempt to settle at Tingri in southern Tibet, because of property disputes, the Sherpas crossed into the valleys of eastern Nepal below Everest.

Most Westerners associate the Sherpas with mountain-climbing expeditions. But traditionally they were traders, herders, and subsistence farmers who spent their summers in Tibet and winters in Nepal, until they discovered the potato. Now settled mainly in the lush area of Solu, east of Kathmandu, potatoes are their main crop. Trekking and climbing services also provide financial compensation, since their former success as middlemen between Nepalese and Tibetan traders ended with the Chinese take-over of Tibet.

The Sherpas speak a dialect close to Tibetan, and are devotees of the Tibetan form of Buddhism, with its roots in the pre-Buddhist faith of Bon.

ABOVE LEFT — *A wheel of life Mandala.*

ABOVE RIGHT — *A Thankha.*

RIGHT — *A Tibetan monastery near Bodhinath.*

34

LEFT — *Votive lamps of burning ghee on an altar.*

BELOW — *A cauldron of ghee (clarified butter) is being prepared.*

BUDDHIST RITUAL OBJECTS:

THANKHAS are religious paintings on canvas, silk, or paper, done according to strict canonical rules, and consecrated by a high lama. They are hung in temples or at family altars, or carried by monks in religious procession.

Called "banners" or "scrolls," because they can be rolled up when not in use, they depict a deity or deities, or scenes from the lives of Buddha, and are often used for teaching. When used as an aid in meditation, the designs are usually geometric, symbolic maps of psychological energies and mental qualities.

MONASTIC MUSIC may be considered an iconography in sound. Its everchanging notes symbolize the transitoriness of all things. The sounds affect the psyche so as to render one more receptive to the Truth.

WHEEL OF LIFE often called the Round of Existence, or Transmigration. The wheel is clutched by a demon, symbolizing impermanence. In the hub of the wheel are a cock, snake, and pig, symbolic of the three cardinal sins of Buddhism, lust, anger, and ignorance.

The body of the wheel is divided into six segments which depict the different worlds of rebirth, dependent on one's karma. The top three segments are good destinies: gods, demigods, and humans. The bottom three are bad destinies: animals, hell, and ghosts.

In the outer rim are twelve scenes showing the causes which govern transmigration. (See: Dependent Origination, p. 17).

ABOVE — *Shiva-lingam and yoni, fertility symbols of Shiva at Pashupatinath temples on the banks of the Bagmati.*

ABOVE RIGHT — *Cremation ghats on Bhagmati River.*

RIGHT — *Pashupatinath Hindu temple.*

LEFT — *Bhairao Nath Hindu temple at Bhadgaon.*

BELOW LEFT — *Children in front of temple.*

BELOW — *Playful children swing in the New Year in traditional ritual.*

LEFT — *A nomad camp near Tingri in western Tibet.*

BELOW — *Nyang River valley under cultivation near Gyantse.*

TIBET

Tibet's history can be traced back to about 200 B.C. when nomadic tribes, largely of non-Chinese Ch'iang stock from eastern central Asia, began arriving and set up small fiefdoms. In 600 A.D. the strongest chieftain, ruler of Yarlung Valley, declared himself king.

The Tibetans were the paramount power in Asia between the seventh and ninth centuries, occupying strategic points on the Central Asian trade routes and invading China's borderlands, even capturing the capital, Sian, in 763.

All the surrounding countries were Buddhist, but the Tibetans still practiced a shamanistic religion called Bon. [See box, p. 40] It was not until 641 A.D. that Buddhism was introduced to Tibet, and at first was only a court religion.

Song-tsan-gam-po, known as the first of the three "religious kings," married a Chinese princess of the T'ang dynasty. A devout Buddhist, she brought an image of the Buddha with her to Lhasa, and to house it the King built the Jo-khang temple. According to Tibetan chronicles, he also married a Buddhist Nepalese princess. Traditionally, the two princesses are known respectively as the White Tara and Green Tara.

King Song-tsan-gam-po sent his minister to India in search of a script to suit their language. He returned with an adaptation of a northern Gupta alphabet, [See box, p. 41] and Tibetan scholars trained in India began translating the Sanskrit Buddhist texts.

In the eighth century the second "religious king," Tri-song-de-tsen, powerfully reinforced Buddhism. He was the builder of Samye, the first Tibetan monastery to train monks. Legend

THE BON-PO'S:

Pre-Buddhist Tibetans were shamanists, who believed in divine kingship, local divinities such as mountain-gods, gods of the soil and the elements, and serpent-deities who inhabit streams and springs. They thought that if the divinities were not properly propitiated, disease and death would result.

The shaman-priest, who invoked the various divinities and made offerings to them, was was known as the *Bon-po* ('Invoker') and *Shen* ('Sacrificer'). There was much borrowing between Bon practice and Buddhist belief over the centuries.

The Buddhist converts kept many local beliefs in the spirit world, simply counting their indigenous Bon gods as 'protectors' of Buddhism. The *Nyingma-pa* (Ancient Ones) sect adapted many Bon rituals to its Buddhist needs. The State Oracle, one of the most important Bon-po functions under the early kings, was later reintroduced by the Gelug-pas. In turn, the Bon-pos paid honor to the Buddhist gods and absorbed much Buddhist theory and practice. At the same time, their shamans continued to perform rites for ordinary villagers and nomads in practical matters, similar to the Brahmins' function in India and Nepal.

The head of Bonpo tantric deity at Gyantse.

STYLES OF TIBETAN SCRIPT: Dbu-can, Dbu-med, Khyug-yig, 'Phags-pa.

A mani stone inscribed with the mantra of the Buddha Avalokita (in Tibetan, Chenrezi, reincarnated in the Dalai Lamas), "O the Jewel in the Lotus" (Om Mani Padme Hum).

Seal script called "Phags-pa" after its Tibetan monk originator; a lingua franca style designed for Khubilai Khan's empire.

Capital letters contrasted with combined lower-case (no-head:Dbu-med) letters and "short-hand" (swift-writing: Khyug-yig).

SCRIPTURES:
KANJUR AND TENGYUR

The Tibetan canon of scriptures is called the *Kanjur* (Buddha-word) and *Tengyur* (Commentary) and includes the Three Baskets of the Theravada tradition (Vinaya, Sutra, Abhidharma) as well as many additional Mahayana sutras and the Tantras. The Tantric texts are placed at the beginning of the Tibetan Canon and form the largest segment. The first printed edition was done in Peking in 1411.

A rocky moonscape near Tingri.

says that when evil spirits kept preventing its completion, the King invited the revered pandit, Padmasambhava, to come from Swat. He quelled the spirits with his magic and mysticism.

Padmasambhava introduced the Tantric form of Buddhism, making use of the common ground between Buddhist tantric rites and certain practices of the Bon-pos. With Tantrism he gained wide popular devotion, which the court Buddhism, with its emphasis on monasticism and academic matters, had not produced.

The third "religious king", Ralpachan, was also a great patron of Buddhism. But in 836 his brother, Langdarma, a Bon-po, murdered him, and taking power, thoroughly persecuted Buddhism. Six years later a monk subsequently assassinated King Langdarma. The Tibetan kingdom broke up, because of feuding in the royal lineage, and the descendants migrated to western and eastern Tibet. Early Buddhism declined for almost 150 years.

The gently rolling hills of Swat in northwest Pakistan, site of ancient Buddhist ruins and home of Padmasambhava, pictured below.

Its rebirth began in 978, when kings in Western Tibet began inviting Buddhist teachers to come from India, Kashmir, and Swat. Tibetan scholars went to India to study at the great Buddhist universities and returned with large numbers of sutras and tantras to be translated from Sanskrit.

Between the middle of the eleventh century to the end of the twelfth, all Tibetan religious sects, except the Gelug-pa, had appeared. Great teachers and ascetics passed on the revitalized religion directly to their disciples, founding innumerable monastic centers. This flowering of Buddhist life was based on the general principles of Theravada, Mahayana, and Tantrayana. The differences between the sects was based on the particular spiritual emphases or mystical traditions of their founders.

Buddhism now existed in its own right in Tibet. Conversely, in India, the land of its birth, Buddhism had virtually disappeared.

MAIN TIBETAN BUDDHIST SECTS:

The word "sect" is generally used to describe the different Tibetan monastic orders and their lay-followers.

The *NYINGMA-PA* (Ancient Ones) sect grew out of the eighth century tradition of Padmasambhava, the most well known of the Tantric masters. His disciples claim direct transmissions of his original teachings. To support their later doctrines they "discovered" buried texts, purportedly hidden by Padmasambhava until the Tibetans were spiritually "ready" for them. Magical rites, yoga exercises and meditation are stressed. Unlike the celibate monks, married tantric priests associated themselves with the everyday life of the people. Their most well-known scripture is the *Tibetan Book of the Dead*.

The *KADAM-PA* (Bound-by-Command) sect evolved into the Gelug-pa in the fourteenth century, but its history begins in the eleventh.

Following the break-up of the Tibetan kingdom in 842, Buddhist teachers and yogins lacked all noble patronage and centralized guidance. Generally speaking, Buddhism had degenerated into extreme forms of Tantrism. Then in 1042 the western kings succeeded in bringing a revered Indian pandit, Atisha, to Tibet and he began the restoration of the original Mahayana teachings. He helped unite the practices of monks and yogins, stressing that both were necessary for higher Tantric practices, which aimed at Buddhahood here and now.

Atisha's followers founded the Kadam-pa sect, but their return to basic Buddhist monastic life — abstention from marriage, intoxicants, travel and the possession of money — had little appeal for the majority of Tibetans, who were more interested in magic to make their crops grow or the rain fall.

The *SAKYA-PA* (place name: Yellow Earth) was founded in 1034 and dominated Tibet with Mongol patronage for centuries.

One of their best-known scholars, 'Phags-pa, invented a universal script for his Mongol patrons that could be used for the Mongolian, Chinese, and Tibetan languages to serve Kublai Khan's great empire. [See Box on Script p. 41].

Another Sakya scholar and great translator of the 11th century was Drog-mi. While attending the monastic university at Vikramashila in northern India with many other aspiring Tibetans, he was initiated into Tantra. The *Hevajra Tantra*, which he translated into Tibetan, subsequently became one of the basic Sakya texts.

A teaching, called "The Way and its Fruit," is the basic training process used by this sect to achieve Enlightenment in a single life: right views, meditation, informed ritual action and fulfillment through Tantra.

Atisha, the revered Indian pandit who went to Tibet in 1042 and began the restoration of the original Mahayana teachings.

The *KAGYU-PA*, (Oral-Lineage) was founded in the 11th century by Marpa, a householder and translator, who also studied in India under Tantric yogins. The hermit Milarepa, his most famous disciple, became Tibet's most beloved saint and poet, with his *One Hundred Thousand Songs.* Milarepa in turn transmitted his meditation technique to Gampo-pa.

Because of the different emphases of various teachers, this sect split into many branches. One of them, the Druk-pa, became the most prominent in Bhutan.

The *DRUK-PA* (Dragon) was created at the end of the twelfth century, and the succession of its head abbot was by inheritance. A number of buried texts (gter-ma) were "discovered," and these esoteric treatises formed the particular teachings of the Druk-pa school. Eventually, the whole of Bhutan took its name, "Druk-yul" (Dragon Country), from the sect, when the head abbot also became the secular ruler of the country.

At first, this branch of the Kagyu-pas appealed only to people who wanted to be simple mendicants, intent on salvation through solitary meditation. They did not want to be members of large communities studying Buddhist scholasticism. But later, that side developed too.

The *KARMA-PA* (Deed/Action) is another branch of the Kagyu-pa sect, founded at the end of the 12th century by one of Gampo-pa's disciples. The Karma-pas had no wealthy patron, as did the other orders, but drew their support from a wide range of nomads and landed families in the neighborhood of their monasteries.

Several lines of reincarnating lamas developed in the fourteenth century, such as the Zhva-mar (Red Hat), and the Zhva-nag (Black Hat), with whom the concept of reincarnating lamas originated. This was soon adopted by other Tibetan sects. The best-known example is the Dalai Lama of the Gelug-pa order.

The *GELUG-PA*, (Virtuous-Ones), was founded by Tsong-kha-pa (1357-1419), a scholar-monk who restored celibacy and insisted on thorough academic training in the monasteries, following the main lines of Atisha and the Kadam-pas.

In Lhasa there are three great Gelug-pa monasteries: Ganden, founded in 1409, Drepung, founded in 1416, and Sera, founded in 1419. In 1447, the first Dalai Lama built Tashilhunpo Monastery in Shigatse, the home of the Panchen Lama.

The fifth Dalai Lama, head of the Gelugpa sect, became the spiritual and eventually temporal ruler of all Tibet in 1642.

At the beginning of the thirteenth century, two great events were to affect Tibet. One was the Moslem advance across northern India, resulting in the destruction of all the great Buddhist universities that had been the well springs of Tibetan scholarship. The other was the murderous course of the Mongols and their conquest of China. In 1207, Genghiz Khan

OPPOSITE — *Nyethang, near Lhasa, where relics of Atisha are enshrined.*

OPPOSITE BELOW — *Milarepa, Tibet's mystic poet-saint, holding a hand to ear to catch the sound of emptiness. A painting in the Sintoka Dzong in Bhutan.*

BELOW — *A painting of Tsongkhapa at Tashilhunpo, amid a thousand Buddhas.*

demanded submission from the Tibetans, but refrained from invasion. The Tibetans piously claim that it was Genghiz's interest in learning about their Buddhism that spared them. Whatever the reason, Tibet was the only country in central and northern Asia to escape the Mongol slaughter.

In 1239 Genghiz's successor, Godan, did send raiding parties into the country. Impressed by the grand lamas, Godan sent for a Tibetan representative, and a Sakya lama was chosen. This lama made full submission to Godan on behalf of Tibet, and was appointed Regent to his court. The Sakya Lama's nephew and successor, 'Phags-pa, [See box, p. 41] was made vassal-ruler of Tibet by Kubilai Khan, who by 1263 was chief of all the Mongols and Emperor of China.

At the same time, Kublai became a devoted patron of Buddhism. That marked the beginning of the unusual relationship between Tibet and China known as 'Patron-Priest.' Religious guidance for the Mongol Emperor of China was provided by Tibetan monks in exchange for the Emperor's political protection of the rulers of Tibet, who were in effect the predominant grand lamas. The only comparison in the West might be that of the relationship between the Popes and Holy Roman Emperors. However, the ramifications of that unwritten bond remain today, with the Chinese claim that Tibet has always been a part of China.

Thus, Tibet was administratively restructured under the Mongols. And the grand lamas of the Sakya order claimed the authority of 'Kings of Tibet,' even though they had to reside at the Mongol court,

Many monastic sects, aware of the Sakyas' gain from their original act of submission to a branch of the Mongols, sought patronage from other Mongol chiefs. Each hoped to make its monastery more powerful so that its prelate would become supreme.

After the Mongol dynasty fell to the Mings in 1368, the Mongols returned to Mongolia, and there was no longer any fixed relationship between China and Tibet.

BUDDHA REINCARNATION: "TULKU'S"

"Tulku" (Apparent Body) is the Tibetan name for a specific reincarnated Buddha or Bodhisattva.

All Mahayana Buddhists believe that the countless Buddhas or Bodhisattvas "incarnate," that is, return in human form for the sake of helping others, but no one knows who or where they are. It is only Tibetan Buddhists who believe that a Buddha-reincarnation can be ascertained in a particular person.

Celibate monks had only the generosity of the faithful, or the inheritances of entering novices, to enhance a monastery's wealth. Such a need probably started the custom of finding an abbot's specific reincarnation.

When an abbot died, the monks would discover that he had been reborn as the child of a rich and noble family, and bring him to the monastery for the training necessary for their newly reincarnated abbot. One of the Kagyu-pa sects, the Karma-pa, was the first to use this practice.

But as religious credibility grew in the culture, it was believed that the abbots of monasteries were actually incarnating Buddhas or Bodhisattvas. Thus the discovery of successors — Buddhas appearing out of compassion for all creatures — had greater urgency and prestige than the original custom.

The Gelug-pa order claims that its supreme abbot, the Dalai Lama, is the reincarnation of Avalokita, the Bodhisattva of Compassion, appearing now for the 14th time for the sake of the Tibetan people.

ABOVE — *Ruins of Gyantse Dzong beside the great monastery.*

BELOW — *Another view of the extensive ruins.*

OPPOSITE — *A view inside the Gyantse Dzong showing typical Tibetan windows.*

Two hundred years later, the Grand Lama of the Gelug-pa order, Sonam Gyatso (1543-1588) accepted an invitation to visit the chief of the Tumed Mongols, Altan Khan. It was Altan who bestowed the title of "Dalai Lama" on Sonam. "Dalai" means "Ocean" (of Wisdom). This title was applied posthumously to Sonam's two preceding hierarchs, as well as to the succeeding reincarnations of the head of the Gelug-pa sect. This friendly association was a political stroke for now that the Gelug-pas were allied with the Mongols they were no longer purely religious. They had become a political-religious force, as great as the Sakyas had been earlier.

The Gelug-pas' position with the Mongols was further strengthened when Sonam's reincarnation was discovered in Altan Khan's great-grandson. But while the Gelug-pas were escorting the fourth Dalai Lama from Mongolia to the Jo-khang Temple in Lhasa, there were already signs of opposition from the other orders. The Red Hat branch of the Karma-pas was especially insulting, which resulted in growing enmity between the Gelug-pas and Karma-pas. In 1616, that Dalai Lama died at the age of twenty-five, probably by poison.

In 1642, the Gelug-pa's ally, Gushri Khan, leader of the Qosot Mongols, defeated the Karma-pas' ally, the King of Tsang in southern Tibet. Gushri made himself king of all Tibet, and installed as spiritual ruler the "Great Fifth" Dalai Lama, builder of the Potala. After Gushri died however, his successor paid little attention to Tibet. Thus, the fifth Dalai Lama became both the political and religious ruler, and henceforth, Tibet was an independent theocratic kingdom.

The sixth Dalai Lama was such a weak ruler, preferring to write poetry and enjoy life, that a regent took over. This regent favored closer relations with the Dzungar Mongols, who were hostile to both the Manchu dynasty (now rulers of China) and the Qosot Mongols, whose chief was Lha-bzang Khan. In 1706, however, the Manchus and Qosots marched on Lhasa, killed the regent, and deported the sixth Dalai Lama to China but he died enroute under suspicious circumstances.

ABOVE — *Fortress of King Karma Teng-skyong.*

LEFT — *The Tashilhunpo Temple housing the giant Buddha Maitreya.*

OPPOSITE — *The head of the Maitreya image, 83 feet tall, looks benignly on worshippers at its feet.*

Lha-bzang Khan, now undisputed ruler of Tibet, installed in the Potala a puppet Dalai Lama, whom the Tibetan people refused. Instead, they found the true incarnation in eastern Tibet, as foretold in one of the poems by his predecessor, the sixth Dalai Lama. For safe-keeping, the child was taken to Kumbum monastery in the Kokonor region.

Then the Dzungar Mongols killed Lha-bzang Khan, aided by the Gelug-pas who had not forgiven him for removing the Sixth Dalai Lama, thereby reducing their power. The puppet was deported to China, and in 1720 the Manchu army escorted the rightful seventh Dalai Lama to Lhasa.

After his death a new government position was officially created, that of Regent. It was for the purpose of filling the 20-year interregnum after a Dalai Lama died, when the new reincarnation had yet to be discovered, educated, and reach his majority before resuming power.

Thus began a 130-year rule by Regents. The eighth Dalai Lama was uninterested in ruling, the ninth and tenth never assumed power, and the eleventh and twelfth ruled only short periods before their deaths.

The 13th Dalai Lama (1876-1933), the first outstanding one since the "Great Fifth", was forced to flee Tibet twice. In 1904 he went to Mongolia to escape invading British troops, and in 1910 he went to India to escape the Manchus, who were overthrown the following year by the army of the People's Republic of China.

The 14th and present Dalai Lama, Tenzin Gyatso, was born in 1935 in northeast Tibet and brought to Lhasa in 1940. The 1950 invasion of eastern Tibet by the army of the People's Republic of China made it necessary to empower him when he was only fifteen years old. In March 1959, during a Tibetan revolt against the Chinese take-over of their whole country, the Dalai Lama escaped to India, where he remains in exile.

TOP — *A detail of doorway construction at Tashilhunpo Monastery.*

ABOVE — *A swastika, ancient Aryan benediction symbol, carved in the floor entering the Maitreya Temple.*

PANCHEN LAMA

After the Dalai Lama, the Panchen Lama is the second highest ranking "tulku" of Tibet. The title and position began in the 17th century when the Fifth Dalai Lama installed his revered teacher as the first incarnate Panchen Lama (Great Scholar-Lama).

The Panchen Lama is the Senior Abbot at Tashilhunpo, the Gelug-pa monastery at Shigatse, and considered by Tibetans to be the reincarnation of the Buddha Amitabha. The seventh incarnation died in 1989.

ABOVE — *A wall shrine to the goddess Tara at Tashilhunpo.*

RIGHT — *A solid brass handle on a door at the Tashilhunpo Monastery.*

Yab-yum; (lit., "mother-father") are figures of deities in sexual embrace, illustrating the essential unity of opposites (e.g. Samsara-Nirvana or finite-infinite), and symbolize the ecstacy of the disciple's Awakening. The images are sculptured or painted on silk or hand-made paper.

RIGHT — *A prayer flag with the Lucky Horse symbol and mantras.*

BELOW — *A lone monk out of nowhere circumambulates a cairn and prayerflags at high altitude.*

OPPOSITE PAGE — *The Tingri Dzong ruins and monastery town at sunrise.*

EARLY MISSIONARIES

In 1624, two Jesuits, Antonio Andrade and Manuel Marques, were dispatched from a mission in Agra to Tsaparang, the capital of Guge, western Tibet, to explore mission possibilities there. They were the first Europeans in Tibet, and the Guge king received them so warmly that Andrade quickly returned to Agra for more reinforcements. The local Buddhist monks, however, opposed the Christians. They even went so far as to instigate an attack on Guge by the neighboring king of Ladakh.

In 1629, Andrade was summoned to Goa to become Provincial. The mission in Tsaparang continued for awhile, with eleven Jesuits coming and going from Agra. It was closed in 1641, however, because of hardships and few conversions.

During that period Andrade's optimistic reports had aroused hopes of a mission in central Tibet as well. Consequently, two Portuguese Jesuits, Estavao Cacella and Joao Cabral, were dispatched from India and made their way through Bhutan, the first Europeans in that country. In 1628 they arrived at Shigatse, then the capital of central Tibet, and were welcomed by the king, Karma Ten-kyong. It was this king who, in 1642, was overthrown by Mongol troops supporting his enemy, the Fifth Dalai Lama.

While in Shigatse, the Jesuits were able to get news of their confreres in western Tibet from the Tsaparang monks studying at Tashilhunpo, the Panchen Lama's monastery.

Cabral soon went back to India, via Nepal, and reported enthusiastically about his findings. Cacella remained in Shigatse for a year and a half and then went to Bihar in June 1629. He returned to Shigatse in September, but was so ill that he died a week later. King Karma Ten-kyong expressed his regrets and sent word to Cabral, still in India, urging him to return. Although he did so in 1631, the mission was soon closed, being considered too dangerous.

Almost a century later, March 18, 1716, an

OPPOSITE — *Yamdrock Lake south of Lhasa.*

BELOW — *Lalung Leh Pass*

BELOW RIGHT — *Karo Pass before descending to the Tsangpo River at Lhasa.*

Italian Jesuit, Ippolito Desideri, arrived in Lhasa. His strenuous journey started in Delhi, then continued through Kashmir and Ladakh. Near Gartok, in western Tibet, he joined a friendly Mongol caravan. During the five-month journey across the roof of the world, Desideri learned the Tibetan language. In Lhasa he won the confidence of Lha-bzang Khan, the Mongol king who held the Dalai Lama's throne from 1706 to 1717. With royal support, and the encouragement of Gelug-pa monks, Desideri studied Buddhist scriptures and was able to enter into debates with the prelates.

During his five years in Tibet, Desideri wrote a 700-page treatise in classical Tibetan on karma and rebirth and the Mahayana teaching on Emptiness. In 1721 he was recalled by Rome and left Tibet for Agra, via Nepal. His subsequent "Account of Thibet" was Europe's most complete and accurate description of the country, its people, and customs until modern times.

OPPOSITE — *The Kumbum (Thousand Buddha) Temple at Gyantse Monastery.*

ABOVE — *Tibetan youngsters at Gyantse.*

RIGHT— *Prayer flag pole at Gyantse Monastery.*

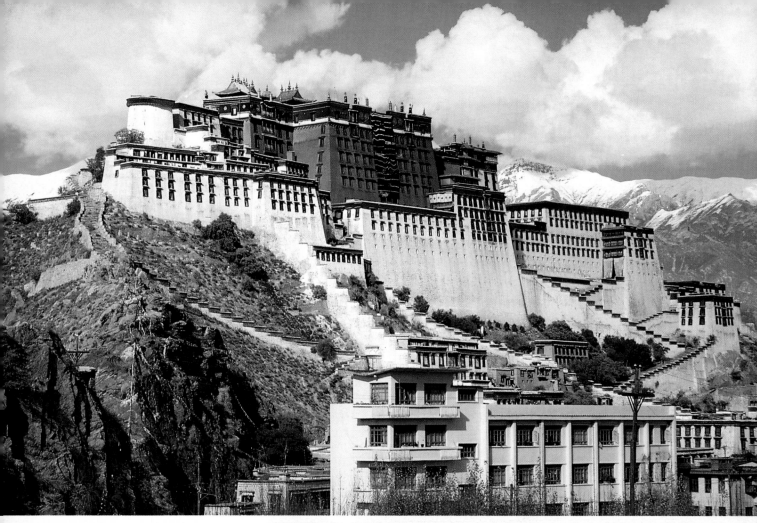

ABOVE — *The Potala with new Chinese apartments in the foreground.*

RIGHT — *Stairways enter the nine-foot thick walls to proceed to inner courts and higher storeys.*

ABOVE — *Gilded roofs atop the Potala mark tombs of previous Dalai Lamas.*

UPPER RIGHT — *An outer staircase leads up to the Potala entrances.*

RIGHT — *A little girl devotee prays at a shrine on the stairway.*

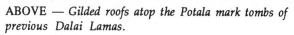

RIGHT — *The entrance to the Jokhang.*

BELOW — *Worshippers entering the Jokhang.*

SEARCHING FOR THE REINCARNATION OF THE DALAI LAMA

Following the death of a Dalai Lama, a group of elder monk-statesmen looks for signs or portents which will help in discovering his rebirth. For instance, the Dalai Lama may have made indicative statements during his lifetime, or he may have died with his head facing a certain direction. Meditative visions by special lamas are interpreted as guides. The State Oracle is consulted.

When fairly certain of where the rebirth took place, the men start their journey, carrying with them many of the deceased Dalai Lama's personal objects — such as sandals, begging bowl, or rosary. Upon finding a likely family with an exceptional child, born within nine months of the Dalai Lama's death, the child is shown his personal effects, as well as careful duplicates. If the child chooses the authentic items, it is a further convincing sign that he may indeed be the reincarnation.

After tests to determine physical fitness, intelligence, and the ability to remember events from his previous existence, the child is brought to Lhasa, along with his whole family, which is ennobled. From then on, he is given years of strict academic and monastic training. At the age of eighteen, he assumes the religio-political power of the office of Dalai Lama.

TOP — *Barkhor, the "walk-around," bazaar encircling the Jokhang.*

ABOVE — *A distant view of the Potala from the roof of the Jokhang.*

RIGHT— *His Holiness, the Dalai Lama and Nancy Gettelman at Dharamsala, India, 1965.*

OPPOSITE — *Pilgrims line up to enter Norbulingkha.*

LEFT — *The Dalai Lama's pavilion at Norbulingkha, the summer palace.*

SIKKIM

Sikkim, the size of Yellowstone National Park, was formerly a semi-autonomous kingdom but is now part of India.

For centuries, a main trade route from the Gangetic Plains of India traversed this beautiful, vertical country through the snows of the Natu La, the lowest pass of the Himalaya, into Tibet. Monsoon rains and a mild climate combine to make ideal growing conditions for hundreds of species of orchids and rhododendrons, as well as verdant forests and terraced farming.

Sikkim's earliest inhabitants, the Lepchas, came from the direction of Assam and Burma. Now Buddhist, originally they were Bon worshipers. The rest of the population, approximately 180,000 people, is made up of Bhutias, Tibetan stock, who are traders and herdsmen in the north and farmers elsewhere; Sherpas, found mainly in the west and who, like the Bhutias and Lepchas, are Buddhists; plus a

ABOVE LEFT — *A stall in downtown Gangtok in monsoon season.*

ABOVE RIGHT — *Terraced hillside outside Gangtok.*

OPPOSITE — *Gangtok, the capital of Sikkim.*

BELOW — *Road to Gangtok: a steep mountain on one side with an abyss on the other.*

few Hindu Indian traders in the south. The Nepalis, also Hindus, now constitute the largest group.

Little is known of Sikkim's political history prior to the mid-17th century. Tradition does hold that Padmasambhava visited Sikkim in the 8th century. Unlike Tibet, however, Buddhism was not adopted by most of the population until the 17th century, when they were influenced by Tibetan monks fleeing the religious and political upheavals in their own country to the safety of Sikkim and Bhutan.

Most of the Buddhist pioneer missionary work appears to have been done by the Nyingma-pa sect, judging from the earliest monasteries which date from around the time the Namgyal dynasty was founded. Three refugee Nyingma-pa lamas crowned the first "consecrated" ruler.

That was in 1642, the same year the Gelug-pas' fifth Dalai Lama became Tibet's religious ruler. While Sikkim acknowledged him as spiritual head, and lamas were sent for training to Lhasa's three most important Gelug-pa monasteries — Ganden, Sera and Drepung — there were, nevertheless, no Gelug-pa monasteries built in Sikkim until after the Chinese take-over of Tibet in 1959. Possibly, because Gelug-pa monasteries were frequently centers of political influence, the Namgyal rulers were endeavoring to protect Sikkim's independence.

The Nyingma-pa monasteries far outnumbered any of the others, and their lamas were the royal priests for the Namgyals. But, since the 18th century, when the fourth ruler, Gyurme Namgyal, made an extended pilgrimage to Tibet, the family has also been closely associated with the Karma-pas. Gyurme Namgyal was so impressed with that sect that upon his return he built three Karma-pa monasteries, all affiliated with one near Lhasa.

After the Chinese take-over, Sikkim and Bhutan were no longer able to send their monks to Tibet for further studies, and consequently have expanded their own religious training. At the same time they keep in touch with the Dalai Lama, living in India, as well as other Buddhist centers in India and Nepal.

TOP — *A Tibetan woman displays her wares in the bazaar at Gangtok.*

ABOVE — *A tailor at his sewing machine.*

TOP — *The market is a gathering place for various occupations and populations.*

ABOVE — *A Tibetan with fine embroidered hat approaches Gangtok.*

The Namgyal royal family traces its ancestry back to an Indian ruling house in a small hill state of what is now Himachal Pradesh. Around the ninth century, according to Namgyal traditions, one of the family migrated from India to Kham, in eastern Tibet, and established his rule over a small principality.

In the 13th century, a Namgyal descendant made a pilgrimage to a Sakya monastery in Tsang, western Tibet, married the ruler's daughter, and later established his authority over the Chumbi Valley. During the next 250 years the Namgyals remained in the Chumbi Valley, establishing close relations with some of Sikkim's Lepcha chieftains.

Toward the end of the sixteenth century, Guru Tashito married the daughter of an influential chieftain from Gangtok, an important trading center, and the Namgyal family moved to Sikkim. Though Guru Tashito is considered by the Sikkimese to be the first Namgyal ruler, his political authority was limited to a small area around Gangtok and the Chumbi Valley.

The Namgyal kingdom was founded upon the support of a number of Bhutia (Tibetan) families who had accompanied Guru Tashi to Sikkim. He was also supported by many of the Lepchas and Tsong (people other than Lepchas and Bhutias). During the reign of the second Chogyal (religious king), the State Council included representatives of those three leading family groups at both the central and local levels. Ministers at the Court ("kajis") were appointed from their ranks.

Guru Tashi's great-grandson, Phuntsog Namgyal, became the first "consecrated" ruler of modern Sikkim in 1642. He established what was probably the first centralized administrative system in the eastern Himalaya. Already in control of present-day Sikkim and the Chumbi Valley in Tibet, he expanded his boundaries to include the area of Nepal east of the Kosi River, as well as Darjeeling district, some of the plains area in India, and the Ha Valley in western Bhutan.

The Chogyal was the head of the Buddhist establishment in Sikkim and considered a

TOP — *A palace gate with Lepcha guards.*

ABOVE — *Hope Cooke in Sikkimese dress modified for traveling.*

The Cabinet pays obeisance to the Chogyal before he and Hope Cooke leave on a trip to India, 1965.

TOP — *The palace is designed like a comfortable English country house.*

LEFT — *The Chogyal, holding his and Hope Cooke's son, Palden.*

71

CLOCKWISE FROM LEFT — *A Tibetan woman spins her prayer wheel and says her rosary. The chapel on the palace grounds where Hope Cooke and the Chogyal were married. A monk holds a Tibetan religious book and rosary on his lap.*

manifestation of the Tantric bodhisattva Vajrapani. He had full temporal and spiritual powers, unlike the divided authorities of the Dharma Raja and Deb Raja system in Bhutan. His succession was on a hereditary basis, rather than by incarnation, and the coronation ceremonies were conducted by the head lama of Sikkim's foremost Nyingma-pa monastery.

The Namgyals chose their wives from prominent Tibetan families. This was true of the late Chogyal and his first wife. Then in 1963, when widowed, he married an American, Hope Cooke.

By the end of the 18th century, the power of the British presence in India had changed the political situation throughout the Himalayan countries. Except for the initial period of expansion after the Namgyal dynasty was founded, Sikkim was constantly assailed by its stronger neighbors. And it was able to maintain some degree of independence only because of its neighbors' rivalries, and the British wish to keep the state a "buffer."

In 1888, the British established a political officer at Gangtok, confirming Sikkim as a protectorate of the British Raj. This greatly reduced the Chogyal's power, further weakened by a landlord-lessee system, whereby the lands "leased" to an official during his service remained in the kajis' hands, instead of being retained by the Court. Another problem was the extensive Nepalese settlement which, by the end of the 19th century, had become the largest ethnic population in Sikkim.

All of this resulted in an internal power struggle, with familial and communal divisions, and in 1975 Sikkim acceded as a state to the Indian federal system. The Chogyal died in 1981.

The Institute of Tibetology was built by the late Chogyal to preserve Tibetan culture, and to house the manuscripts and sacred objects brought by Tibetan refugees fleeing the Chinese in 1959. Tibetology scholars from all over the world have studied at the Institute, designed in typical Tibetan architecture.

73

BHUTAN

WESTERN BHUTAN: THIMPU AND PARO VALLEYS

Bhutan, the easternmost kingdom of the Buddhist Himalaya, derives its name from the Indian word *Bhotanta,* meaning "limits of Tibet," and refers to the boundaries of Tibet's cultural and political influence. In *Dzong-kha* ("language of the dzongs," used by educated Bhutanese) the country is called *Druk-yul,* Dragon Country.

The early Bhutanese, like other Himalayan peoples, were animists, worshipping the spirits of mountains, trees, stones, and caves. To propitiate these sometimes benevolent, but more often malevolent, spirits, shamans applied magic and ritual.

During Tibet's paramountcy in central Asia, 7th to 9th century, Bhutan was widely colonized. When the Tibetan kingdom broke up in 842, many soldiers garrisoned at Bhutanese outposts refused to go back to Tibet's civil turmoil and persecution of Buddhism. In addition to the soldiers, a number of lamas and their followers migrated to the refuge of Bhutan's hidden valleys, transplanting their Tibetan sects to the mountain kingdom.

TOP — *The Punakha Dzong at the confluence of the Pho Chu (river) and Mo Chu.*

ABOVE — *Two little girls at Thimphu wearing typical Bhutanese bokhu.*

OPPOSITE PAGE — *The Paro Dzong in western Bhutan.*

ABOVE — *Sintoka Dzong: Blue Raven on which the Shabdrung dreamt he would fly to Bhutan from Tibet.*

RIGHT — *The Tashichho Dzong at Thimphu, now a permanent seat of government, including a large monastic community and home of Bhutan's head lama.*

Bhutan has no written record of its early history before unification in the 17th century, although Tibetan monks mention it in their religious histories of the "Ancient Period" (11th to 16th centuries). Some religious information is found in the *gter ma* (rediscovered treasures) attributed to Padmasambhava who, it is believed, visited Bhutan in the 8th century.   To this day he is revered as "Guru Rinpoche" (Precious Teacher) because he first brought Buddhism to the Bhutanese.

The groundwork for Bhutan's eventual emergence as a distinct nation was laid in 13th century Tibet, when the Drug-pa sect, a branch of the Kagyud-pas, founded a new monastic centre and religious school in Tsang. Ten generations later the Drug-pa began the reincarnation tradition, choosing their abbots from important clans who gave them patronage.

Their most famous incarnation, Padma Kar-po, was born in the 16th century and became became head abbot of the sect. Known as a "universal" man, whose scholarship can be compared to that of the Fifth Dalai Lama, he wrote an extensive history of the Druk-pa sect in 1575 and systematized their centuries of teaching.

After Padma dkar-po's death a dispute arose between two candidates from different clans, each claiming to be the Abbot's reincarnation. One of the two was Nga-wang Nam-gyal, who fled Tibet in 1616 to escape the jealous competition. In Bhutan he won acceptance as the true incarnation among the Drug-pas already there and founded the "Southern Druk-pa" sect. It is from this religious sect that the country takes it name.

Nga-wang Nam-gyal, given the honorific title of *Shabdrung*, built many great fortress-monasteries (dzongs) and was responsible for the unification of Bhutan. To assist him in governing its nine major valleys, the Shabdrung appointed "penlops" (governors of territories) and "dzongpons" (governors of dzongs). He was the first Dharma Raja ("Religious Ruler"), later delegating temporal affairs to another high-ranking lama, the Deb Raja ("Secular Ruler"). Thus began the spiritual-temporal rule by reincarnating lama-kings and ministers which lasted nearly three hundred years.

It was this first Shabdrung whom Cacella and Cabral met in 1627 in Paro, western Bhutan. The two Portuguese Jesuits were on their way from India, their destination Shigatse and the court of King Karma Ten-kyong. This king was the

TAKSANG (TIGER'S NEST)

According to tradition, in the 8th century Padmasambhava visited Bhutan's thirteen "Tiger's Nests." They were named "Tiger" because, in Buddhist iconography, Guru Rinpoche's customary vehicle or mount is a tiger. In addition, Bhutan is famous for the Bengal tigers which roamed high into its valleys from the Duars of Bengal and Assam.

The most famous "Tiger's Nest" is a nearly-inaccessible shrine and tiny hermitage-monastery a few miles northwest of Paro. It was here that Milarepa, the beloved Tibetan mystic and poet, wrote of his meditations in four of his 100,000 Poems.

ABOVE — *The Tiger Nest.*

ABOVE RIGHT — *Cave altar at Tiger Nest.*

RIGHT — *The Abbot's cell at Tiger's Nest, chilly in winter.*

OPPOSITE PAGE — *The Tiger Nest Monastery (Taksang Gompa).*

Shabdrung's enemy, who mounted three separate invasions of Bhutan — all of them unsuccessful.

The Shabdrung detained the priests in Paro, giving as his reason the treacherous journey to Tibet. From Cabral's letters to his superior, however, it is clear that the real reason was the prestige the foreigners' presence brought to the Bhutanese court. As a result, it was almost a year before Cacella and Cabral were able to continue on to Shigatse, secretly aided by a monk opposed to the Shabdrung.

A large part of Bhutan's history during the last three hundred and fifty years consists of the struggle for power among the nobles. In theory, the Deb Raja was elected by the penlops and dzongpons but, in truth, the office was held by the strongest of the penlops.

In 1907 the most powerful of the penlops, Ugyen Wangchuck, became the Deb Raja. In 1917, he was proclaimed the first hereditary king and knighted by the British. During his grandson's reign no reincarnation of the Dharma Raja was found, and the spiritual-temporal rule came to an end. Ugyen Wangchuck's great-grandson, King Jigme Singye Wangchuck, is the present ruler of Bhutan.

TOP — *The Sintoka Dzong with Blue Raven.*

LEFT — *Boy monks at Thimphu monastery.*

OPPOSITE TOP — *A not uncommon phallic symbol on a home next to Thimphu bazaar.*

OPPOSITE RIGHT — *The Governor of the Punaka Dzong and district (with a sword at his side) and Fr. William Mackey, advisor to the Bhutan school system.*

RIGHT — *Punakha Dzong.*
BELOW — *An inscription on the King's stupa at Thimpu.*
OPPOSITE — *King's stupa at Thimphu, a Bhutanese in
tennis shoes is circumambulating the stupa.*

BELOW — *The chorten at the King's stupa.*

DZONGS

Until recently there were no towns in Bhutan. Consequently, the centers of activity for each of the nine major valleys were the dzongs. Though no longer involved in warfare between the lords of the valleys, these monastery-fortresses are still the focus of civil adminitration and all religious life.

From Tashichho Dzong in Thimphu, the now permanent royal capital, to Punakha and Wangdi Phodrang in the center of Bhutan, to Tashigang Dzong in the east, the Bhutanese contribute time and labor for the upkeep of the dzongs in their particular valley.

EASTERN BHUTAN

RIGHT — *Narthang consists of a few bamboo sided and roofed shops at a widening in the road halfway to Sherubtse School from the Assam/Bhutan border.*

BELOW — *A mani wall astride the footpath through a deep cultivated valley where rhododendrons bloom.*

LEFT — *Antlike lines of Nepali road workers carry crushed rock up five hundred feet in a hillside bucket brigade.*

BELOW LEFT — *A nobleman's house. The animals sleep on the first floor, providing warmth for the family on the second. The third floor is used for storage.*

BELOW — *A mani wall and chortens. The author has the wall on her left; in correct circumambulations the wall is kept on one's right, thus going clockwise.*

SHERUBTSE SCHOOL

Sherubtse School, the first modern school in the country, is situated in eastern Bhutan, 40 miles from the Tibet border at an altitude of 7,000 feet. It was built in 1968 by the late king, Jigme Dorji Wangchuk, as a measure to stop the "brain drain" — students leaving Bhutan to get an education.

After the Chinese incursion into India from Tibet in 1962, the Indian government was anxious to have access to the Tibetan border. Consequently, an agreement was reached with the King whereby, in exchange for allowing the building of a military road through his country, Indian Army engineers would construct a complete modern school facility near Tashigang Dzong.

To oversee this step into twentieth century education, the King invited a Canadian Jesuit teacher to come from Darjeeling, with the understanding that no Christian proselytizing would be permitted. The new educational system has since flowered into several centers across the country, administered by Bhutanese. All the schools focus on agricultural and trade needs and jealously guard Bhutan's cultural and religious identity.

ABOVE LEFT — *Students gather in front of the school's clock tower.*

ABOVE RIGHT — *A modern auditorium where the students have adapted Shakespeare's plays to their culture.*

ABOVE — *Some of the modern cement block buildings that make up Sherubtse school.*

OPPOSITE PAGE — *Students in national dress march from Sherbutse School, built in 1963 by Indian engineers. It was the first twentieth-century school in Bhutan. In exchange for the building of it, the late King gave permission to India to build a military road from the Assam/Bhutan border to Tibet.*

LEFT — *Tashigang Dzong.*

BELOW — *The Abbot of Tashigang Dzong, 1969, holding ritual bell and dorje, sits in lotus position in his top floor eyrie.*

ABOVE — *The gate to the Tashigang Dzong.*

BELOW — *The outer court of the Tashigang Dzong. Homes of lay officials are outside the Dzong courtyard. A sixty-foot prayerflag waves in the breeze.*

LEFT — *A Bhutanese in colorful bokhu, with required ceremonial scarf draped properly for Dzong visit, enters the single main entrance of Tashigang with the author. In their party of four, she and the other two women were the first western women in Eastern Bhutan, 1969.*

BELOW — *A view of the inner court.*

MASKS and SACRED DANCES

Masks are worn in the sacred dances, considered an active meditation. The dances are much like the West's medieval morality plays in that they teach, or tell a story, for the purpose of helping people along the path to Awakening. For the already initiated, higher awareness is important in the integrating and harmonizing of bodily postures (mudras), chanting the liturgy (mantras), and activating the higher internal energies (mind).

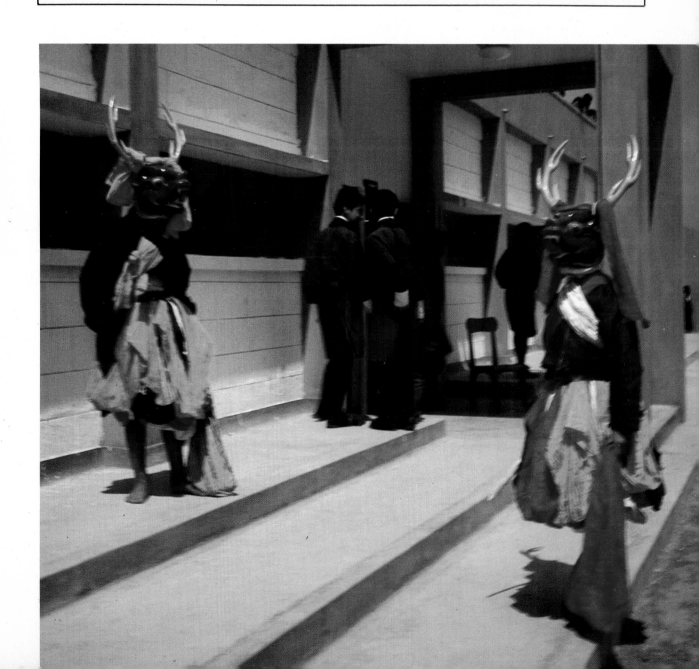

LEFT — *Bhotia highlanders in homespun yak wool and felt "rain caps" and yakskin boots.*

BELOW — *New hamlet under construction in the valley next to Tashigang Dzong.*

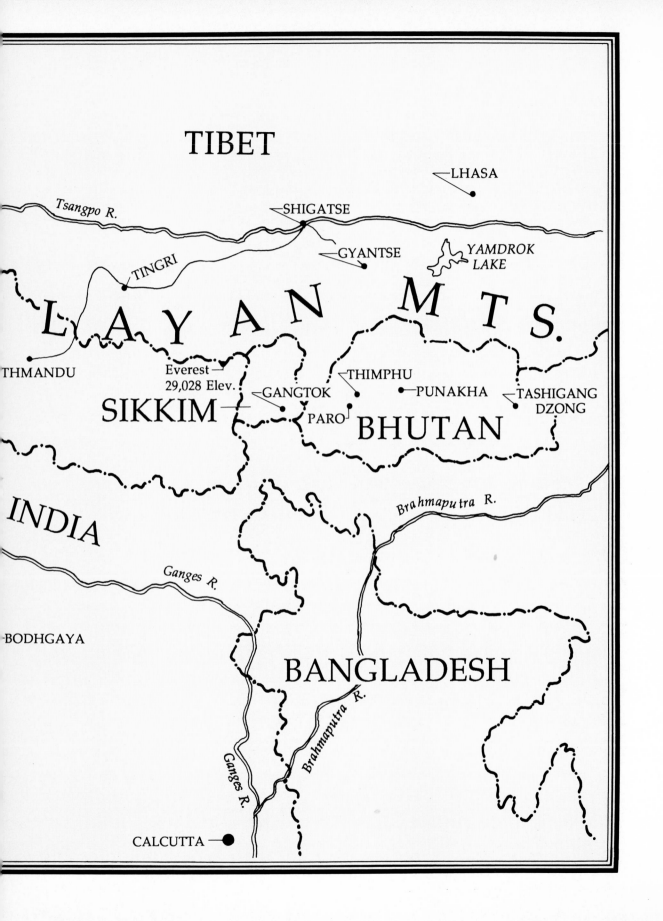

PHOTOGRAPH CREDITS BY PAGE
Front matter pages — Pages 5, 7 and 9 by Rev. Richard Sherburne, S.J.

INDIA

NANCY GETTELMAN
Pages 12,
16 (Wheel of life),
18 (A town near Bombay),
21 (Monks in Darjeeling),

Rev. RICHARD SHERBURNE, S.J.
Pages 10, 11, 13, 14, 15,
16 (Boy monks),
16 (Woman of Shudra caste),
18 (Sidewalk tea vendor), 19,
21 (Old and new)

NEPAL

NANCY GETTELMAN
Pages 23 (Former Malla palace), 25, 28,
31 (Stucco archway),
34 (A Tibetan monastery),
35 (A cauldron of ghee),
36 (Cremations ghats),
36 (Hindu temple),
37 (Hindu temple),
37 (Children in front of temple)

Rev. RICHARD SHERBURNE, S.J.
Pages 22, 23 (Annapurna), 24, 26,
27, 29,
30 (Brahmin),
31 (Monks), 32, 33,
34 (Wheel of life mandala),
34 (Thankha),
35 (Votive lamps),
36 (Shiva-lingam),
37 (Playful children swing)

DAVID BARAGA
Page 30 (Gurkhas)

TIBET

NANCY GETTELMAN
Page 65 (The Dalai Lama)

Rev. RICHARD SHERBURNE, S.J.
Pages 38, 39, 40, 41, 42, 43, 46, 47,
48, 49, 50, 51, 52, 53, 54, 55, 56,
57, 58, 59, 60, 61, 62, 63, 64, 65 (Dalai Lama's Pavilion)

SIKKIM

NANCY GETTELMAN
Pages 66, 67, 68, 69, 70, 71,
72, and 73

BHUTAN

NANCY GETTELMAN
Pages 84,
85 (Nepali road workers),
85 (A nobleman's house), 86, 87, 89,
90 (Gate to Tashigang Dzong), 93

Rev. RICHARD SHERBURNE, S.J.
Pages 74, 75, 76, 77, 78, 79, 80, 81,
82, 83, 85 (Mani wall), 88,
90 (The outer court), 91

DAVID LOOSE
Page 81 (The Governor of Punaka Dzong)

Design by Roz Pape, Seattle
Composition by Peter MacKenzie, Seattle
in 10/12 Palatino with display lines
    in Zapf Chancery
Printed on Sterling Gloss Book
    and perfect bound by
Victory Graphics, Milwaukee